Introduction

WELCOME to the second look at "Suffolk 100 Years Ago." This collection of photographs was donated to the Ipswich Museum by Ipswich printers W.S Cowell in 1948. They are the original images used to produce a series of picture post-cards in the "Fairlight Series." After the printing plates were made, the photographs were probably thought to be of little further use and printer's notes were written on the images in red wax pen. With the use of computer technology, undreamt of by the original photographers, I have restored the photographs to their original condition.

The photographs were taken on large glass negatives exposed in brass bound wooden tripod mounted cameras. Photographers were a rare sight in the villages and people gathered to watch them at work. Although photography was first patented in 1839 it was not until commercially produced dry plates became available in the 1880s that photographers started to record topographic scenes on a large scale. The Royal Mail did not permit the sending of picture post-cards until 1894.

The trend to send a picture post-card from a visit to another town soon became a huge industry in the Edwardian era. It was also fashionable to collect cards in special albums. This was from a time before local newspapers carried photographs. The cinema was in its infancy and there few other means to see images. The post-cards often recorded news and other events. A dramatic image of a fire or disaster would often arrive with an unconnected message "Arrived safely, wish you were here" etcetera.

This series of photographs appear to be from three separate photographers commissioned by the publishers.

Most of the cards were produced to a standard 5 ½ x 3 ½ inches from November 1899. Although mass produced tourist scenes were produced by the lithographic printing process many photographers would sell actual photographic prints of much smaller print runs. Some small events and street scenes would be sold by the dozen.

The cards were often sold from a village post-office and they regularly feature in the views. Post card photographic paper was produced until the 1960s and a single card of a family member or event with "post card" and a space for a stamp on the back is not uncommon.

I am sure you will enjoy this second look at Suffolk from a time when life was at a different pace brought to you by Archant, the publishers of the East Anglian Daily Times, Evening Star, other newspapers and magazines and Ipswich Borough Museum and Galleries.

Dave Kindred 2005.

Design and reprographic work by Design Studio, Press House, 30 Lower Brook Street, Ipswich Suffolk, IP4 1AN.
Published by Archant Suffolk, Press House, Lower Brook Street, Ipswich, Suffolk IP4 1AN.
Printed by William Gibbons and Sons Limited, Willenhall.

FELIXSTOWE: Children enjoying themselves on the beach near Cobbold's Point (background). By today's standards the children are overdressed. On the left is the Fludyer's Arms hotel.

2

FELIXSTOWE: The Orwell Hotel opened in 1898 opposite the town's new Felixstowe Town rail station, which was opened the same year by the Great Eastern Railway Company. The original station was Felixstowe Beach which opened in 1877. A roundabout is now in the foreground of this view and the hotel is the Elizabeth Orwell Hotel.

Suffolk 100 years ago

FELIXSTOWE: An elegantly dressed Edwardian group enjoying the summer sunshine in Hamilton Gardens. The lady makes sure her skin stayed fashionably white under the shade of her parasol. The pier is in the background.

FELIXSTOWE: The promenade and beach from near Sea Road looking towards the pier. Well clothed children were enjoying traditional beach fun.

FELIXSTOWE: Donkey rides for young visitors. Everybody is wearing a hat, an important fashion item for Edwardians of all ages.

FELIXSTOWE: Wolsey Gardens from Hamilton Gardens. Bent Hill is off to the left. Halfway along on the right at the corner of Stanley Road is Eastwood Ho College, a private school.

FELIXSTOWE: A boy watches the photographer working with a large plate camera from the promenade near the Town Hall. This picture was taken looking towards Cobbold's Point (background).

FELIXSTOWE BEACH NO 1.   FAIRLIGHT SERIES.

FELIXSTOWE: A busy beach and promenade from near the Spa Pavilion. In the background is the Felix Hotel, which was opened in 1903 by the Hon Douglas Tollemache. The hotel had 250 bedrooms. In 1919 the hotel was acquired by the Great Eastern Railway Company.

FELIXSTOWE: The pier, which was opened by the Coastal Development Corporation in July 1905. It was 2,640 feet long and was visited by the steamer service from London. The first vessel to bring passengers was the paddle steamer Woolwich Belle.

FELIXSTOWE: Convalescent Hill from the pier. In the centre is the Town Hall, which opened in September 1892, built at a cost of £1800.

FELIXSTOWE: The promenade from near the pier looking towards Convalescent Hill and the Town Hall. The two-mile promenade was built in 1902.

FELIXSTOWE: The main route to the sea front from the Felixstowe Town station was along Hamilton Road. The section of road from Orwell Road to Bent Hill was then known as Victoria Parade.

Suffolk 100 years ago

13

NACTON: The rail bridge at Orwell Station. The rail line from Westerfield to Felixstowe was financed by George Tomline, a wealthy land owner whose home was at Orwell Park Nacton. The line opened in 1877 and included this station close to George Tomline's home.

NACTON: A lady at her cottage gate watches the photographer at work. This would have been a rare sight a century ago. The arrival of the rail line to the village around thirty years earlier would have brought travel opportunities unheard of a generation before.

CRETINGHAM: St Peter's Church register dates from 1558. It is built of stone and flint in Gothic style with a chancel, nave, south porch and embattled western tower.

HENLEY.   FAIRLIGHT S. ...

HENLEY: The scattered village around four miles north of Ipswich had a population of 243 in the census of 1911, a few years after this picture was taken. The main road from Ipswich to Hemingstone was then just a dirt track and motor vehicles were a very rare sight. The house on the left is at the corner of Bell's Cross Road, opposite the Henley Cross Keys public house.

Suffolk 100 years ago

BRIGHTWELL: The main route from Woodbridge to Felixstowe was unmade when the photographer visited. In the centre is the village blacksmith's workshop. The population of the village in the 1911 census was 82.

WOODBRIDGE: The Thoroughfare from Cumberland Street. On the left at the corner of Church Street is The Cross public house, which was established in 1652. On the right at the corner of Quay Street is The Crown Hotel. The sign above the hotel says it is "a family and commercial hotel."

SECKFORD ST WOODBRIDGE NO I. FAIRLIGHT SERIES.

WOODBRIDGE: Everybody has stopped to pose for the photographer in this view of Seckford Street. This view is looking towards Queen's Head Lane, which is off to the right.

WOODBRIDGE: Seckford Street. The only traffic in this view looking towards Market Hill was a lone horse and wagon. On the left is the Queen's Head public house and Queen's Head Lane. The public house is now a private home.

WOODBRIDGE: A view from the rail station looking towards Quay Street. The Station Hotel (now The Anchor) is at the corner of Station Street and Quay Street. On the right are the premises of Arthur John Garnham, jobmaster, and funeral carriage proprietor.

WOODBRIDGE: Market Hill with the Shire Hall on the extreme right. The White Horse inn is halfway along on the left. The tower of St Mary the Virgin church is top left.

MARKET HILL WOODBRIDGE NO 3 FAIRLIGHT SERIES.

WOODBRIDGE: Market Hill. The building in the centre with the sign on the front is the Gardener's Arms public house. One of the gas lamps supplied by the Woodbridge Gas Light and Coke Company located at the Quay is in the centre.

WOODBRIDGE: Shire Hall has been the focal point of the town since it was built in 1575 by Thomas Seckford, Master of the court of Requests to Queen Elizabeth I.

WOODBRIDGE: New Street with The Olde Bell and Steelyard, a sixteenth century inn on the right. The building features a steelyard. The word comes from the German for weighbridge, used to weigh wagons of barley.

WOODBRIDGE: New Street looking towards Market Hill. The public house on the right is The Case is Altered. The Olde Bell and Steelyard on the left. In the road is one of the town's postmen.

WOODBRIDGE: Theatre Street looking towards Market Hill. On the right is Edgar Goldsmith's "smith and farrier". The Royal William Inn is on the left.

WOODBRIDGE: A road sweeper cleaning traffic free Church Street. This view is from near the gates of St Mary's church, looking towards Quay Street.

WOODBRIDGE: Drybridge Hill with a group of children on the roadside watching the photographer at work. The girl opposite on the pavement has moved during the exposure.

WOODBRIDGE: The Thoroughfare with the Royal Oak public house on the left. The sign offers accommodation for cyclists, which was a relatively new leisure pursuit when this photograph was taken.

CHERRY TREE INN WOODBRIDGE FAIRLIGHT SERIES

WOODBRIDGE: The Cherry Tree Inn, Cumberland Street. The entrance to Notcutt's nursery is now on the left of this view.

BROMESWELL. The village is on the main route from Woodbridge to Orford. Transport a century ago was mainly horse drawn. A smartly dressed coachman, probably from a nearby estate passes through on a buggy.

MELTON: Four children in typical Edwardian dress at Melton Terrace on a winter's day. The terrace is close to Ufford Park Hotel Golf & Leisure centre. This was then the main road from Ipswich to Lowestoft.

WILFORD BRIDGE

FAIRLIGHT SERIES

MELTON: Wilford Bridge over the River Deben on a winter's day. The road is now the busy A1152 carrying hundreds of vehicles every day.

THE POST OFFICE CLOPTON.   FAIRLIGHT SERIES,

CLOPTON: The post office was a vital link for the 325 residents listed in the 1911 census although the nearest post office dealing with telegraphs and money orders was three miles away at Grundisburgh.

DEBACH: The Public Elementary School, which was built in 1858 for 78 children. The population in the 1911 census was 130. This fine Victorian school building is now a private house.

EYKE: This row of cottages is opposite All Saints church. The furthest building is the Elephant and Castle public house.

EYKE: Most of the windmill on the left was demolished around 1910. The village postman is in the centre.

RUSHMERE: A traffic free village then completely separate from Ipswich. The ivy covered building on the right is the Baptist Church built in 1859. The furthest buildings on the right of the street at the corner of Holly Lane have been demolished.

RUSHMERE: The Street was an unmade track when this view was taken. The ivy covered Baptist Church halfway along the street on the right is featured in the picture on page 40. When the picture was taken the village had a blacksmith, wind and steam mill and an elementary school for 120 children, built in 1846.

RUSHMERE: This row of cottages is in the then aptly named Seven Cottages Lane. Only six of the modernised cottages remain today.

RUSHMERE: A pair of postmen outside the village post-office. The other man in the picture has a tricycle from the Victorian era.

MARTLESHAM: This was the main road from Ipswich to Woodbridge with a brick bridge taking mostly horse drawn traffic over the River Fynn. There was an alternative route through the river.

MARTLESHAM: Traditional travellers with their caravans. Travellers and their children would often find seasonal work on farms.

MARTLESHAM: These cottages stand at the crossroads of School Lane (right) and Bealings Road (left). The Red Lion public house is behind the trees on the left.

MARTLESHAM: The Red Lion public house from the School Lane. The public house dates back to the late 1500's. It was a coaching inn also used as an overnight stop for the Royal Mail.

SAXMUNDHAM: Church Street with the premises of John Freeman, blacksmith (centre left).

SAXMUNDHAM: High Street looking north with the rail bridge carrying the Ipswich to Lowestoft line. The gas lamp on the right was supplied by the Saxmundham Gas Company Ltd. Market place is off to the left.

UFFORD: Barrack Lane from near the bridge (see page 51). The Avenue is off to the right. When the photographer visited the village had an elementary school, a grocer, boot repairer, blacksmith, wheelwright and post office.

Suffolk 100 years ago

UFFORD: What remains of the charming little bridge and ford in Barrack Lane is now lost in undergrowth. The tower of St Mary the Virgin is on the left of this view. The church has a magnificently carved font cover dating from the fifteenth century. The church register dates from 1558.

UFFORD: The main road from Ipswich to Lowestoft on a winter's day. Spring Lane is off to the right (between the telegraph poles) in this view is looking north.

UFFORD: The windows of this cottage were open on a warm summer's day. Woman and children have gathered to pose by their ivy covered homes.

GRACECHURCH STREET, DEBENHAM.

DEBENHAM: Gracechurch Street, which was lit after dark by gas lamps supplied by the Debenham Gas Light Company in Water lane. The gas works were built in 1858.

DEBENHAM: Three girls stand by a Victorian School building. The town had two schools, the elementary senior, which was established in 1879 and the elementary junior, which was erected in 1838 and enlarged in 1895. The population of Debenham in the 1911 census was 1196.

BRAMFORD: Bramford Water Mill in Mill Lane was powered by the River Gipping. This view is from near St Mary's Church gate. Ship Lane runs across the picture.

BRAMFORD: Fitzgerald Road from the junction with Vicarage Lane. All of the houses near the camera on the left have been replaced. The village was a thriving community with a blacksmith, wheelwright, harness maker, baker, rail station and police station.

SPROUGHTON: Two boys on the bank of the River Gipping. In the background is the tower of All Saints Church. The tower contains a clock presented in commemoration of Queen Victoria's Diamond Jubilee in 1897.

SPROUGHTON: The road bridge over the River Gipping. The village then had a grocer, stonemason and post office all operating from the same premises, also a blacksmith, wheelwright and a working water mill.

SPROUGHTON: A group of children, with girls in pinafore dresses, huddle by a gateway in High Street. This is the main road to Washbrook.

Suffolk 100 years ago

SPROUGHTON: A stable lad with a horse and buggy in the grounds of Sproughton Hall, which is opposite Church Lane in Lower Street.

BLAKENHAM: The lock gates on the River Gipping. In the background is the tower of St Mary's Church. Fifteen locks were completed in 1793 opening the River Gipping for navigation between Ipswich and Stowmarket. The work took three years.

CREETING LOCK. FAIRLIGHT SERIES.

CREETING: The lock gates where barges loaded with cargo, towed by horses, once passed through. The opening of the rail line saw trade decline on the river and when this picture was taken the fertiliser factory at Bramford was where most barge trade from Ipswich ended.

NEEDHAM MARKET: Boys playing on the bank of the River Gipping. Behind the trees in the centre is Hawks Mill. This brick mill was built in 1884. The building is now converted for residential use.

Suffolk 100 years ago

NEEDHAM MARKET: A pleasant walk along the tow path of the River Gipping for an elegantly dressed Edwardian lady and her dog.

LITTLE BLAKENHAM: The rectory and St Mary's Church with girls enjoying the winter sunshine.

MENDLESHAM: Front Street with A and M Cutting's shop on the right. Cutting's provided the village with an amazing range of services. They were grocers, provisions dealers, ironmongers, hop and malt merchants, house furnishers, general and fancy drapers, boot and shoe dealers, general outfitters, newsagents, agents for Lloyds Bank, Norwich Union Insurance and Perth Dye Works.

PEASENHALL: St Michael's Church with its embattled tower and four pinnacles has a register dating from 1558. The nave and chancel were taken down and rebuilt between 1860 and 1861. The work was paid for by Mr J W Brook of Sibton Park.

EASTON: The White Horse public house (right) with the tower of All Saints Church on the left where the register dates from 1561.

RAYDON: Children are able to play in the traffic free village street. When this photograph was taken the village had a rail station on the Hadleigh branch line, a blacksmith, a police station, a hurdle maker, post office, boot maker and two public houses.

CODDENHAM: The Live and Let Live public house is on the left of this view of High Street. There was a Roman settlement here called Combretonium, which became Coddenham in Saxon times.

GRUNDISBURGH: The main road into the village from Woodbridge was an unmade track.

GRUNDISBURGH: Cottages on Rose Hill with the tower of St Mary's Church in the background.

GRUNDISBURGH

FAIRLIGHT SERIES

GRUNDISBURGH: The remoteness of Edwardian village life would mean that trips to towns like Woodbridge, Ipswich or a visit to the coast were a rare event. Some folk never left their village throughout their life.

GRUNDISBURGH: St Mary's Church from the village green. The brick church tower was built in 1751 with funds left by Mr Robert Thinge. The church was restored internally in 1874. The register dates from 1540.

WALDRINGFIELD: Three generations in the garden of an ivy covered cottage.

Suffolk 100 years ago

WALDRINGFIELD: Cottages viewed from School Road. The village school (behind the camera) built in 1874 for the parish of Waldringfield, Hemley and Newbourne was enlarged in 1892 to take 88 pupils.

WICKHAM MARKET: Rackham's water and steam Mill from the main road to Lowestoft. This view has changed very little is the past century although the chimney on the right has gone.

STOWMARKET: Ipswich Street with the Dukes Head public house on the left. In the centre background is the tower and spire of St Peter and St Mary Church. The gas lamp on the right was supplied by the Stowmarket Gas Light and Coke Company.

COMBS FORD.

FAIRLIGHT SERIES.

STOWMARKET: Combs Ford with carts in the street opposite the Magpie Inn.

STOWMARKET: Combs Ford with the rare sight of a motor car on Poplar Hill. On the right is the Volunteers public house. The shop on the left is Arthur Purr's grocery store. The Magpie public house is in the centre.

LITTLE BEALINGS: The village blacksmith outside his forge. It is possibly Herbert Ward at work, who traded in the village for many years.

LITTLE BEALINGS: Edwardian girls in smart hats on the bridge over the River Fynn in The Street.

ELMSETT: The teacher's house at the village school, which was built in 1870 at a cost of about £600. The school was enlarged in 1874 to take 100 children.

Suffolk 100 years ago

ELMSETT: Cool summer dresses for these young ladies standing by a smart picket fence outside the village post and telegraph office.

CLAYDON: Residents pose outside their cottages. When this photograph was taken the village was an independent community with a blacksmith, baker, butcher, saddler, carpenter, bricklayer, boot maker and repairer.

Suffolk 100 years ago

BARHAM: The Workhouse served the poor from 1766 to 1925. After finishing as a workhouse the building had several uses including a home for Jewish refugees from Germany including 159 children. Soldiers from both World Wars also had barracks there. It was demolished in 1963.

HINTLESHAM: The main route from Ipswich to Hadleigh from near St Nicholas Church.

TUDDENHAM: A group of youngsters are able to pose in the middle of the road from Ipswich to Grundisburgh without fear of high speed traffic. In the right background is the Fountain public house.

PLAYFORD: The village post office is on the left at the corner of Church Lane. Villagers had to travel to Bealings for money orders or to use the telegraph.

Suffolk 100 years ago

PLAYFORD: The bridge over the River Fynn on a summer's day. This view was taken looking towards Culpho.

CHARSFIELD: A delivery man lets his horse graze by the Baptist Chapel. Trades in the village then included a thatcher, tailor, butcher, shoe maker and repairer and post office.

Suffolk 100 years ago

WESTERFIELD: Most of the girls are wearing pinafore dresses and hats as they pose on a muddy track through the village. The boy is in typical school uniform of the time including boots and cap.

BURSTALL: The Half Moon Inn. Edgar Garrod was the landlord when the photographer visited. The population of Burstall in the 1911 census was 237.

LITTLE STONHAM: St Mary's Church with its embattled tower and a double hammer beam roof which is richly carved with figures of apostles and saints. The church register dates from 1535.

NEWBOURNE: St Mary's Church where the register dates from 1561. The flint tower was restored in 1885 at a cost of £200.

KERSEY: A group of children by the ford in the centre of the picturesque village. In the background is Church Hill with St Mary Church behind the tree.

IPSWICH: Upper Brook Street from the junction with Tacket Street. J Bird's greengrocers shop and Underwood and Son's boot manufacturers, cycle retailers and bag merchants are on the left. Sainsbury's supermarket is now on this site. On the right gas lamps hang outside Great Alexander, clothiers.

Suffolk 100 years ago

IPSWICH: A very busy day on The Cornhill. This view, looking towards Tavern Street, has the Town's main post office, at the corner of Princes Street on the extreme right. Featured are three of the town's electric trams, which came into service in 1903.

WHITTON: This was then a village 2 ½ miles from the centre of Ipswich on the main road to Norwich. In 1903 the electric tram service connected the village to the town and Whitton was the end of the line. On the left is the Maypole public house.

WHITTON: The Maypole public house looking towards Ipswich. This was then the main road from Ipswich to Norwich. This route is now by passed and called, The Old Norwich Road.

WHITTON: The village was swallowed up into Ipswich when new council housing was built in the 1930s. This view is from where White House Road is now off to the left of Norwich Road. Where the group of children are there is now a petrol filling station.

WHITTON: The police station (right) was built in 1903 and the policeman featured is Benjamin Meadows who had his five children living at the station with him. It is probably four of them in the photograph. The station had two cells for local trouble makers.

WHITTON: A large group of children, all in classic Edwardian dress, stand in the main road from Ipswich to Norwich. This view is from the Maypole public house looking towards Whitton Church Lane. The shop in the centre was the village store run by S E Self.

Suffolk 100 years ago